And how?

And how?

A guide to self-care,
self-leadership and purpose

Araceli Higueras

TITLE: *And how?*
AUTHOR: *Araceli Higueras©, 2024*
COMPOSITION: *HakaBooks - Optima 12*
COVER DESIGN: *Hakabooks©*
ILLUSTRATIONS: *Didac Meseguer y Araceli Higueras©*

EDITING AND CORRECTION: *Tu voz en mi pluma*
1st EDITION: *March 2024*
ISBN: *9798320603872*

The total or partial reproduction of this work by any means or procedure, whether electronic or mechanical, computer processing, rental or any form of transfer of rights is prohibited, within the limits established by law and under the legally provided warnings. the work without written authorization of the copyright holders.
All rights reserved.

IMPRIME: *Podiprint*

*I'm going to do like at the Oscars...
I dedicate this book to my mother and father,
my partner and my children... for raising me,
putting up with me and teaching me.*

*This book would not exist without the work of
Natalie Runyon at Thomson Reuters,
the training of Mark Sparrow, the supervision of
Louis Harvey... to name a few of the strongest and
most direct influences I have had.*

INDEX

Who I am? 15

	I		You		They	
1 *The way to be* 17	Confidence	19	Respect	21	Influence	23
2 *Connecting* 25	Speaking	27	Enquiry	29	Reputation	30
3 *Purpose* 31	Intention	33	Consideration	34	Impact	35
4 *Mind power* 39	Awareness	41	Empowerment	43	Change	45
5 *What makes the world go around?* 47	Self-Love	49	Relationships	52	Network	54
6 *Balance* 57	Health	59	Care	60	Service	62
7 *Unstoppable* 65	Sport	67	Energy	68	Momentum	70

Words of gratitude 73
The Author 75

Dear reader,

What you have in your hands is a labour of love. This is a compendium of learning, observations and experiences that I want to share with the world, hoping to make it a better place for all of us.

Each chapter is structured in three parts; we're approaching each topic from three perspectives: I, you and they. That is to say: first person —"my" perspective—, second person —"yours"—, and third person —that of an unknown mass of people.

The reason being I want to talk about what we can do for ourselves, what we may do for the person in front of us, and, last but not least, let us talk about other people that are also important or relevant.

I am influenced by systems thinking and I want to represent systems (and our interdependency) in this way. Furthermore, I hope you'll find topics (actions and learning) easier to tackle in this way.

May you enjoy and be fulfilled. :)

Best wishes,

Araceli

Who am I?

I'm an inquisitive Vitruvian woman with a passion for handcraft, an addiction to sport and a love for learning: languages, science, technology, design, psychology… I confess I don't know what boredom is.

https://www.linkedin.com/in/aracelihigueras/

Perhaps the most important questions are "who are you?" and "who do you want to be?".

#1 The way to be

How do you show up? What do others feel when you are with them and after you left? What are you remembered by?

#1.1 Confidence

At our core, we need a certainty about our abilities that stems from **confidence**. Perhaps I should have written Confidence, with a capital c.

This sort of Confidence can withstand change, can adapt and transform us, and what is around us.

Confidence is not certainty; however, it is clarity, in the sense that it fuels you with determination towards a goal that is explicit and distinct enough for you. It talks to others, convincing and calming them, bringing them along.

What gives you confidence?

Confidence is contextual, and its flip side (in my opinion) is fear of failure. When you have a clear goal and trust in your ability to achieve it: that is confidence.

You need not know *how* or *when*, but you most likely know **why**. Knowing your *why* gives you clarity in your own values, coherence between

And how?

your values and what you are trying to achieve with your objectives.

What to do now?[1]

- Values exercise.
- Goals exercise.

---

1 There are many exercises in search engines. Have a look at this one, for example https://soulsalt.com/list-of-values-and-beliefs/

#1.2 Respect

Being confident doesn't mean being like a bulldozer and stepping over everyone else.

Now that we are in the "second person section", I want to discuss respect as a fundamental way of being towards others, and a human right. We owe and deserve respect.

«*Respect yourself and others will respect you*», **Confucius**

I wanted to dedicate a section to this *way of being* because, although extremely intangible, I find it fundamental. In my opinion, it is related to honour and appreciation. Respect is a strong foundation for relationships and a healthy behaviour partner.

Respect includes:

- Not speaking over others;
- Giving them space to show up as themselves (for example with their gender identity);

And how?

- Not harassing or even molesting physically;
- Asking for consent.

What to do now?

Ask yourself how well you know other people's preferences and whether you take them into account.

#1.3 Influence

Ultimately we're on a mission.

It's important to think about "others", the third person, because, realistically, there's very little that we can do on our own. That's why we live in families, we work in cooperatives or joint enterprises, we 'team up'.

However, what are we *doing*? Are we leading or are we following? I don't believe in leading the whole time. I am also a big fan of "servant leadership". Leaning on a clear shared purpose, a servant leader has the very important role of connecting the team with the organisation's mission and removing impediments.

In my humble opinion, the key to influence is alignment. Unless everyone cares about the same thing, we don't move in the same direction.

And how?

What to do now?

There are so many ways to influence. Body language, verbal language, sales techniques, threats, mind games... You name it.

I believe in honesty, being direct (both in offering help and feedback/opinions). I try to be considerate, but sometimes I'm told that I am simply "brutal".

On the other hand I am forever learning and developing myself on this topic, and, most importantly, reflecting and trying new approaches to make an impact on what I care about.

I recommend you ask for feedback.

#2 Connecting

Imagine a colony of ants building bridges, harvesting, going about their business as a single entity. They need a very strong connection.

#2.1 Speaking

In Clean Language training I was told to do pair exercises that showed me how the quality of my speaking was proportional to the quality of how I was being listened to.

There are many (good) courses on how to speak, and I very much recommend learning the basics to always improve on body language, structure of the message, the use of our breathing and voice, etcetera. Pick vocabulary as specific as possible but understood, make use of silence, project your voice, look in the eyes.

Beyond that, I strongly feel that connecting with the audience is not done purposefully enough. We need to look for ways to make the audience listen to us —and course correct, when what we are doing is not working.

The second concept that deserves more attention than it currently has is our inner dialogue. We speak to ourselves regularly. When we speak to others, we do it better if we don't trip ourselves up in the process (with our internal dialogue).

And how?

What to do now?

Learn communication structures.

Example 1: Problem, solution, benefit.

Example 2: The point you're trying to make, the reason, an example and a re-cap of your point.

Communicate with structure so that the audience can follow you more easily, and remember better what you say.

#2.2 Enquiry

Strong connections happen mainly when there is exchange and understanding. Ask questions to the person in front of you and have an interest in what they are doing, what scares them, makes them happy, worries them, and makes them smile.

There isn't a bullet proof question and you are certainly not going to have a very well packaged answer with all the information. Having an approach of enquiry, however, will pay off, because you will learn from and relate to others.

What to do now?

Make a point of taking the time to ask questions to others (and listen!). Repeat their words to them to make them feel listened to.

Talk a little bit about yourself to turn the conversation into an exchange of ideas, not an inquisition. But focus on asking a variety of questions.

#2.3 Reputation

Ultimately, a lot of what happens to us, many decisions that affect us are made when we are not present. This is where reputation is crucial.

I don't believe in becoming completely hooked on social media, having a strong dependency on what we look like or being involved in any "make believe". In this section, I am talking about having a strong ethical foundation, being honourable, treating others well, working to the best of our ability and communicating in a healthy and relevant way. So that we influence our personal brand, what we are known for.

What to do now?

Keep track of your achievements, ideally in a situation-action-impact format.

Make sure that those who need to know about you have evidence about you. Make your achievements visible to gain credibility.

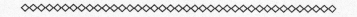

#3 Purpose

Why do you do what you do? Why do you do it the way you do it? What is in it for you? What legacy do you want to leave behind? What would you like to have happened? Are you proud of the end result?

Funny questions, coaching questions, growth mindset questions to gain clarity about our destination, to pave our way and course correct as necessary.

#3.1 Intention

This is the first check-in in my opinion. I'm a strong advocate of assuming "positive intent", also in those actions we take and become most critical of.

Whenever we find ourselves dealing with something we want to change, it is super useful to dig a little and find out what NLP (neurolinguistic programming) calls "the secondary benefits". Always satisfy the underlying benefit of those habits that you want to change, in order not to trip yourself up.

With ambitions and constructive goals, the intention is pure propelling fuel, wind in your sails. Keep it at the forefront of your mind and let it feed you with energy and sometimes even love.

What to do now?

A great exercise is the 5 whys.

And how?

#3.2 Consideration

You have a person in front of you who is different from you. The best thing you can do is take the time to realise where you end up and where they begin. What makes them tick, what they care about, their goals and aspirations. And how that is different from you.

It takes time and consideration. You need to observe, listen and enquire.

In order to build bridges between the present and the future, reality and a goal, we need synergies with others, and these occur when we align ourselves with them.

What to do now?

Find out about your peers' goals, domain knowledge, experience and influence.

#3.3 Impact

Since we are now in the third person section, it would be remiss of me not to draw your attention to how you can achieve your goals by enrolling others, bringing them along for the ride.

You need others to be involved in your plans to make them happen, to execute certain tasks, to "make way" (remove impediments) for things to happen.

Impact when we talk about purpose is closely linked to 1) delegation (those tasks you don't need to do personally) as well as 2) support. For example, organising household chores, childcare, caring for the elderly, and so on.

When I first became a mum and my partner and I were straining under the increased workload (we were both working), one of my friends said "I'm not surprised that you're overstretched, there are two of you doing three jobs". Such a great way of describing it! Take into account the resources and the people necessary to get things done, *#strongertogether*.

And how?

Another story I'd like to share involves giving kudos to Open University UK. When you enrol in a course with them, they want to set you up for success. They want you to understand the effort that studying takes and for you to plan how to make it happen, both by organising your time and by enrolling your family and friends.

In order to be part of a scalable and sustainable initiative, we need the alignment that comes from a shared purpose. This is what I understand as impact.

What to do now?

Make a list of everyone you need and have a clear idea of their role, their level of engagement with your project and their level of influence over other people.

#4 Mind power

How do you want to train your mind to work in your favour?

Our brains are not perfect and trip us up. We have cognitive biases, we oversimplify, we have fears that short-circuit our ability to think rationally.

#4.1 Awareness

《Awareness is curative》 is a very famous quote by **Timothy Gallwey**. You may have heard of (or read) *The Inner Game*, his first and most famous book.

I follow three coaching principles: flexibility, goals and feedback.

It's important to have a clear, unobstructed view of where we want to go (and where we are going, they may not be the same). We are led by our objectives, the other guidance is provided by feedback. Flexibility is your ability to course correct, to change tactics, to persevere or revise your overall strategy when new information comes to light.

Awareness is the growth, the transformation of what we know and what we pay attention to, which allows us to do something we couldn't do before.

Coaching relies on a few beliefs; for example: 1) we have the necessary resources to take on

And how?

the changes we want to embark on, and 2) we can learn along the way.

What to do now?

Please consider journaling. Journaling is the best way I know to gain awareness on those issues where we have a blind spot.

The way we journal depends on our goals and circumstances. A very good neutral recommendation (to turn your journal into action learning) would be to log:

- Your goals.
- What actions do you need to take? (Brainstorming).
- What first step do you commit to take? (When, where and with whom?).
- What support system will you use? (Who will help you?).
- How will you know you have made progress on this objective?

#4.2 Empowerment

Bring those who are with you onto their most useful mental state. Make them feel good about themselves, capable, resourceful. When you do that, they are at their most resourceful and productive state. You build a good experience of what it is being with you, they walk away with a good memory and think of you fondly.

This comes into play after the previous chapters' second person section, since connecting and enquiring take precedence. Hopefully the breadcrumbs that I'm leaving from one chapter to another are becoming apparent.

Small side note: Whenever someone asks for help, turn it into a sign of strength, reframe it as "good collaboration" and delegation skills.

Being powerful doesn't exclude teamwork.

And how?

What to do now?

Take the time to consider how you can make a difference to others.

Actually, we don't often even need to think very hard, since this is not a surprise birthday party: we can ask them. *How can I assist you?* Or make specific suggestions, making sure not to steamroll over more quiet personalities.

Make them feel safe.

#4.3 Change

What might be possible if you created the circumstances for others to systematically be at the top of their game?

I am not talking about taking responsibility for the lives of others. I don't imply that it is simple or that we become the "one trick pony" that dishes out miracle solutions, because there are no unique formulas.

What am I talking about then? I am talking about role modelling, being the change, walking the talk.

Put your money where your mouth is, share your opinion. More importantly, since actions speak louder than words, show up and lead the way being a great example.

And how?

What to do now?

Speak up. Share your journey, your learning and your conclusions.

Unfortunately, sometimes we allow ourselves to strive for some dream-like objectives only after we have seen somebody else attempt or achieve them. Well, if we know that's how the human brain works, let's use it in everybody's favour. Share your achievements and inspire others. :)

#5 What makes the world go around?

The song would say money, and money is certainly important. Unless we resort to barter, money buys us food, clothes, water, light and heat, and a long etcetera.

However, money is only on the surface. All sorts of emotions and desires drive us I would argue in favour of the millennial wisdom of philosophy and mythology. Pride, greed, lust, envy, gluttony, wrath and sloth.

I personally believe we can even go into a deeper level and, underneath it all, there is love at our core.

#5.1 Self-Love

Love yourself. Look after yourself physically and mentally.

Get to know yourself, to understand what "triggers" you.

Speaking for myself purely, I can share what works for me.

Sleep

First, I protect my sleep and, to be more precise, my sleeping hours, as much as possible. So not only do I try to sleep a minimum of hours, but I endeavour to sleep at similar times throughout the week and the year. Regardless of whether I'm on holiday, no matter if it is the weekend, or if the days of the year are long or short...

If you haven't heard about circadian rhythms, I suggest you do some reading about it and how it can affect your performance and wellbeing.

And how?

Sport

A small addendum to this section is sport. I guard my sports time fiercely and prioritise it over many other things. I'm hooked on how I feel when I do sport.

Curiosity and learning

Thirdly, I cultivate an attitude of curiosity. Listening, reading and learning (in general) make me feel very fulfilled. Like the day was worth it. I set myself regular learning goals, some personal, some professional.

Volunteering

The last activity that I want to share here is volunteering. Whether it is at the school board, an employee network or a charity or non-governmental organisation, making yourself available to support your community builds strong bonds and a shared sense of purpose and fairness.

Be on the lookout for opportunities to make things better for others, just for the love of it.

#5 What makes the world go around?

What to do now?

Take a good look at how you spend your days. Log your activities, use your agenda, if you have one, become aware of where you spend your time and *decide* where you want to spend it; carve time and protect it fiercely to make sure you do what you want.

And how?

#5.2 Relationships

I find few things in life more beautiful than connecting with others.

Feeling understood, loved and supported. Being there for others in their time of need.

Sharing work or any type of burden to make it less heavy. I refer to the logistical burdens involved in caring for children or the elderly, to financial responsibilities and, of course, to work projects too.

I don't know about you, but I feel a sense of belonging, something 'clicks' inside me. Part of my mind relaxes and allows the rational part of my brain to get into "the zone" and become more productive.

Examples include telling somebody about a typo, including them in a conversation, or updating them.

What to do now?

Relationships don't look after themselves.

Although some relationships stay very healthy in a dormant state, and wake up fully once you can reunite with your friend "as if you had never been apart", that is not true of every relationship.

Furthermore, being in the same physical space is not enough, it cannot be used to describe what nurturing a relationship is. Thoughtfulness, acts of kindness, and displays of attention and affection are what I am talking about.

Do not take anybody for granted, especially those you care most about.

And how?

#5.3 Network

I love the **African proverb** that says «*it takes a village to raise a child*».

There are so few things that can be accomplished purely by ourselves that it is mind blowing to realise how connected and interdependent we are with each other and nature. What a difference it makes when we are of the same mind.

In this section I want us to think of those we know and find out about their interests, their priorities, the domain of their knowledge, their contacts and level of influence.

What to do now?

Draw a stakeholder map or table. Take some time to better understand those that surround you.

#5 What makes the world go around?

The key of this exercise is to end up understanding how your skills, your ability to add value, and ultimately your mission align with what each person wants and cares about.

It would be overwhelming to think of every single person or contact in our environment. I suggest you start with key people from your family, managers, peers, clients and any decision makers in your main activity.

#6 Balance

How to sustain yourself and ensure you can persevere towards your goal?

How do you do your best to "enjoy the journey"? How to make sure you respect and honour your multiple commitments, satisfy your multiple interests, so that you don't feel life is passing you by?

#6.1 Health

I am not baptised, but I did grow up in Catholic culture, so I recognise the religious connotation of "your body is your temple".

Even if we take our religious glasses off for a minute, I recognise a wisdom in the saying that transcends religion, along the lines of «*mens sana in corpore sano*». To ensure a good journey, look after your body.

Your body is your true partner, your instrument, and your home. Love it, maintain it, embrace it.

What to do now?

Your body changes as time goes by. Keep it moving, stay active, in whatever ways work for you.

Have it checked by professionals (vision, teeth, gynaecological check-ups, etc.) on a regular basis, so that you know everything is well or how to look after it, when something changes.

And how?

#6.2 Care

By now you have seen that every chapter is not about me, myself and I. I also advocate for "the person in front of us". This also extends to physical care.

Keeping the person in front of you (or next to you) and their wellbeing at the forefront of your mind, acting as if you do, engaging them, listening actively to them, with empathy, with questions, with warmth will make them feel better cared for.

Some people do need to take better care of themselves, and I do not intend to disempower them by having somebody else look after them instead.

On the other hand, some people actually need some nudging so they start looking after themselves better. Your questions and your concern will make them feel important. You may even "awake" in them self-awareness and a healthy habit.

What to do now?

What are you comfortable knowing about others? Some of my suggestions are:

Did you sleep well? What can I do for you? Is something on your mind?

We can carry weight for others that we see are struggling, we can make time to have informal conversations and listen to others, without putting our agenda first.

You never know, we can even learn something. :)

And how?

#6.3 Service

There is a Spanish proverb that I live by: «*Haz el bien, sin mirar a quién*». It encourages you not to be constrained by who you are helping or assisting, it's a "just do it" type of message in the context of serving others.

What does service mean to you? To me it means being of value, making a difference. It takes active thinking and an effort to understand what is currently happening, what others need or value. You can ask, of course, but not everyone will feel like asking, "entitled" to what they want, or perhaps they won't be aware of what they need.

This is an active attitude to do what's within our grasp to remove obstacles for others, to share their journeys and to make the world the place where we are proud and happy to live in.

What to do now?

This is about you, your priorities and preferences, and the legacy that you want to leave behind, how you want to be remembered.

This can be a force for good, when you align yourself to goals that go beyond your individual scope there is room for synergies and «*you kill two birds with one stone*».

Map out your immediate environment and understand what happens around you, is there anything lacking? Prioritise your actions on those issues *you* care most about.

#7 Unstoppable

You know what I'm talking about, what gets you 'in the zone' at the speed of light, where almost everything appears effortless and I am tempted to say it's even close to being a pleasure.

Time flies and we bounce back from failure, we "feel the fear"[2], but it doesn't stop us. Stopping is simply not an option, we are 200% convinced of what we're doing, and this unshakable belief makes us a magnet for followers and a force to be reckoned with.

---

[2] Feel the Fear and Do It Anyway is a very famous book by Susan Jeffers.

#7.1 Sport

What makes me unstoppable? Sport.

Looking after my body is one level, but keeping it at its prime, or as good as it gets, that's another story. Sport stimulates my mind enormously, it enhances my self-esteem, makes me happy.

It's such a chemical shot that I can't help but strongly recommend sport to everyone.

What to do now?

Take action: It's up to you, but are you up to exploring what physical activity could suit you?

Taking a walk, yoga, swimming. It doesn't matter. The main thing is that you do something, anything, and that you do it consistently. That's when you reap the benefits.

And how?

#7.2 Energy

How do you show up?

This is a new expression for me, I started hearing it a few years ago in the UK. I suspect it's here to stay, it is very powerful. It originally means turning up or arriving, however, it is used to encourage active management of one's brand and presence. It supports the idea that you can play an active role in how you are perceived and what impact you make.

Showing up is important in diversity and inclusion circles when discussing topics or aspects of your life that are relevant to you, you care about because it conveys support to minorities or communities different from yours.

What to do now?

Are you compartmentalising your life? How is that working for you?

Typically we are more relaxed, feel less on edge and less defensive if we can bring the whole of ourselves at work (or vice versa at home). This does not mean sharing absolutely everything.

I encourage you to find a way to be comfortable with who you are

And how?

#7.3 Momentum

Why not put it in writing? I would like the world to be a better place than it is today. And I believe all of these coaching skills do create a better place for everyone, including those we haven't met or interacted with yet.

And what better way to finish the book than with some wishes to enable others, leading by example, removing obstacles for others, and leaving a meaningful legacy?

That's the meaning of life, if you ask me.

What to do now?

In my humble opinion, it is not necessary to turn our life upside down or to address all the issues in the world. I suggest you pick two or three that are very meaningful to you. It can be draining to take on big topics, so I suggest you limit them. In this way, you avoid spreading yourself too thin.

There are so many things that you can do:

- You can lobby the government.
- You can lobby companies.
- You can raise awareness of others.
- You can start a non-profit organisation or support existing ones.
- You can launch a "social enterprise".

Words of gratitude

Thank you for reading these words.

This is not a long book, but I hope its structure and content have inspired and encouraged you.

Thank you to those who have trained me, worked with me, and accompanied me on my journey, with a mention to **Hakabooks** and **Tu Voz en mi Pluma**.

If you are looking for a coach and you think I could be that coach for you, do not hesitate to reach out to me.

I work with people 1-2-1 or deliver **"How to be the CEO of your career"** workshops.